Table of Contents

Educational Media

rourkeeducationalmedia.com

Mills Haven School

Can you find these words?

clothes

food

shelter

water

Need It or Want It?

Needs are things we can't live without.

food

You need **food.**

4

"I want candy, please."
We don't need candy.

5

water

You need **water**.

"I want soda, please."
We don't need soda.

You need **clothes.**

clothes

"I want a coat like Max's."
We don't need what others have.

You need **shelter**.

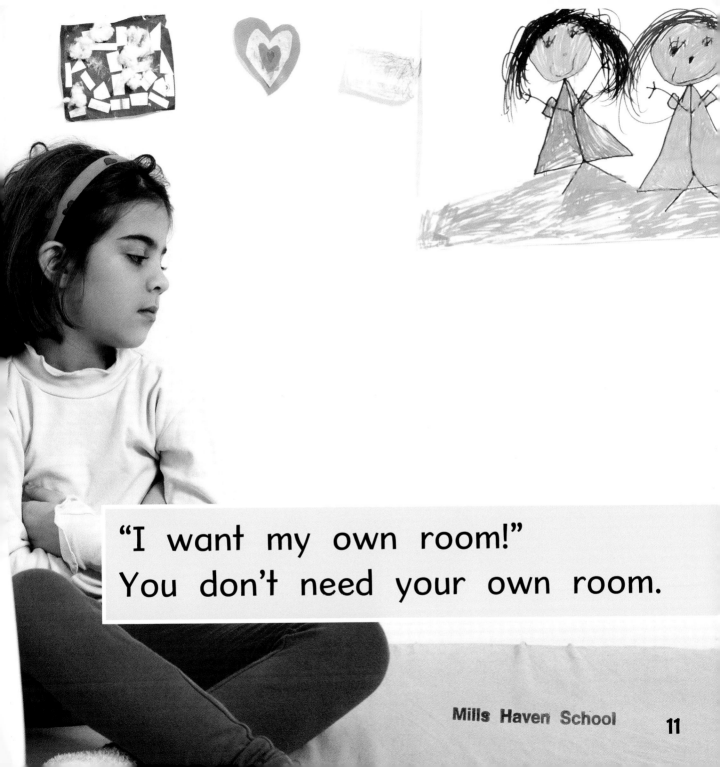

"I want my own room!"
You don't need your own room.

Mills Haven School

You need love.

We need each other!

13

Did you find these words?

You need **clothes**.

You need **food**.

You need **shelter**.

You need **water**.

Photo Glossary

 **clothes** (clohz): Things people wear to cover their bodies.

 **food** (food): Things people and animals eat to stay alive and grow.

 **shelter** (SHEL-tur): A place that protects people and animals from bad weather and danger.

 **water** (WAW-tur): The colorless liquid that falls from the sky as rain.

Index

About the Author

Tammy Brown writes books and teaches teachers how to teach their students to read. She enjoys reading all kinds of books and loves to travel!

© 2019 Rourke Educational Media

All rights reserved. No part of this book may be reproduced or utilized in any form or by any means, electronic or mechanical including photocopying, recording, or by any information storage and retrieval system without permission in writing from the publisher.

www.rourkeeducationalmedia.com

PHOTO CREDITS: Cover, p.7: ©OcusPocus; p.2,8-9,14,15: ©ArtMarie; p.2,4,14,15: ©Steve Debenport; p.2,8-9,14,15: ©Milenko Bokan; p.2,6,14,15: ©baona; p.3: ©Davel5957; p.5: ©Mark Bowden; p.12-13: ©ideabug

Edited by: Keli Sipperley
Cover design by: Kathy Walsh
Interior design by: Rhea Magaro-Wallace

Library of Congress PCN Data
Need It or Want It? / Tammy Brown
(Plants, Animals, and People)
ISBN (hard cover)(alk. paper) 978-1-64156-160-0
ISBN (soft cover) 978-1-64156-216-4
ISBN (e-Book) 978-1-64156-271-3
Library of Congress Control Number: 2017957772

Printed in the United States of America, North Mankato, Minnesota